Baboons

Baboons

survivors of the African continent

Louise Barrett

London, New York, Sydney, Dehli, Paris, Munich, and Johannesburg

Publisher: **Sean Moore**
Editorial director: **LaVonne Carlson**
Project editor: **Barbara Minton**
Editor: **Jennifer Quasha**
Art editor: **Gus Yoo**
Production director: **David Proffit**

First published in 2000 by
BBC Worldwide Ltd,
Woodlands, 80 Wood Lane, London W12 0TT

Text, design and illustrations
© BBC Worldwide Ltd 2000

ISBN 0-7894-7152-3

Produced for BBC Worldwide by Toucan Books Ltd, London

Printed and bound in France by Imprimerie Pollina s.a. - n° 81933-A

Color separations by Imprimerie Pollina s.a.

PICTURE CREDITS:

Page 3 Gerald Cubitt. 6 A.B.P.L./Peter Lillie/Gallo Images. 9 Olive Pearson. 10 Gerald Cubitt. 11 Photo Researchers Inc/C.K. Lorenz. 12 BBC Natural History Unit Picture Library/Richard Du Toit. 13 Oxford Scientific Films/Mark Deeble and Victoria Stone, T; DRK Photo/Anup Shah, B. 14 Photo Researchers Inc/Tom McHugh. 15 Photo Researchers Inc/R. Van Nostrand. 16 Wayne Ford/Wildlife Art Limited. 17 Gerald Cubitt. 18-19 Wayne Ford/Wild life Art Limited. 21 Oxford Scientific Films/Richard Packwood. 22 Ardea/Adrian Warren. 23 NHPA/Ann and Steve Toon. 24 A.B.P.L./Nigel J. Dennis/Gallo Images. 25 BBC Natural History Unit Picture Library/Nick Garbutt. 26 Minden Pictures/ Frans Lanting. 27 DRK Photo/George J. Sanker. 28 Gerald Cubitt. 31 Ardea/ Stefan Meyers. 32 Photo Researchers Inc/Gregory G. Dimijian. 33 Photo Researchers Inc/Renee Lynn. 34 Oxford Scientific Films/Animals Animals/Peter Weiman. 35 Ardea/M.Watson. 36-37 BBC Natural History Unit Picture Library/Richard Du Toit. 38 BBC Natural History Unit Picture Library/Andrew Murray. 39 DRK Photo/David Northcott. 40 Minden Pictures/Konrad Wothe. 41 NHPA/Anthony Bannister. 42 NHPA/Daniel Heuclin, T; DRK Photo/ Thomas Dressler, B. 43 Gallo Images/ M. Harvey. 44-45 NHPA/ A. Warburton and S. Toon. 45 DRK Photo/Anup Shah, TR. 46 NHPA/Nigel J. Dennis. 47 Ardea/Ian Beames. 48 Oxford Scientific Films/Clive Bromhall. 49 Photo Researchers Inc/Tom McHugh. 50 Ardea/C. Clem Haagner. 51 Minden Pictures/ Gerry Ellis. 52 Gallo Images/ M. Harvey. 55 Minden Pictures/Frans Lanting, T; Wayne Ford/Wildlife Art Limited, B. 56 BBC Natural History Unit Picture Library/Anup Shah. 57, 58 A.B.P.L./Peter Lillie/Gallo Images. 59 BBC Natural History Unit Picture Library/Ron O'Connor. 60 NHPA/Daniel Heuclin. 61 BBC Natural History Unit Picture Library/Ron O'Connor. 62 BBC Natural History Unit Picture Library/Anup Shah. 63 NHPA/ M. Harvey. 64-65 Gerald Cubitt. 66 BBC Natural History Unit Picture Library/Anup Shah. 67 NHPA/Peter Pickford. 68 DRK Photo/Tom Brakefield. 69 BBC Natural History Unit Picture Library/Ron O'Connor. 70 Gerald Cubitt. 71 BBC Natural History Unit Picture Library/Anup Shah. 72 Gerald Cubitt. 73 Oxford Scientific Films/Richard Packwood. 74-75 Gallo Images/M. Harvey. 76 BBC Natural History Unit Picture Library/Anup Shah. 79 Premaphotos/Ken Preston-Mafham. 80 Minden Pictures/ Tim Fitzharris. 81 A.B.P.L./Nigel J. Dennis/Gallo Images. 82-83 A.B.P.L./Carol Hughes/ Gallo Images. 84 NHPA/Stephen Krasemann. 85 Oxford Scientific Films/Christian Gazimek/ Okapia. 86 Ardea/Stefan Meyers. 87 BBC Natural History Unit Picture Library/Andrew Murray. 88 Oxford Scientific Films/ Adrian Bailey. 89 A.B.P.L./Nigel J. Dennis. 90 Tom Stack Associates/John Shaw. 91 Oxford Scientific Films/Clive Bromhall. 92 Gerald Cubitt. 93 Photo Researchers/ Rennee Lynn.

Contents

1

THE ADAPTABLE MONKEY

1 THE ADAPTABLE MONKEY

There is just the faintest glow on the horizon and the soft cooing of red-eyed turtle doves begins to fill the still air of the East African savanna. As the sky lightens, the huddled forms of a group of yellow baboons can just be seen among the branches of a grove of acacia trees. Gradually, the baboons begin to stir. The small juveniles are the most active at first. They leave the shelter of their mothers' bodies and seek out their playmates. They chase each other through the trees, crashing through the branches, until they catch each other and engage in energetic wrestling matches.

The adults begin the day more sedately. Soft grunting can be heard as the females begin to groom each other. Sitting close together, they search carefully through their partner's fur for ticks and other parasites. Then a couple of baboons move away from the sleeping site to feed. It is the start of another baboon day.

Previous page: Baboons have wide-ranging diets. This chacma baboon from South Africa feeds on the leaves of a mopane tree.

A DAY IN THE LIFE ...

All baboons across Africa generally begin the day like this. An hour or more can be spent grooming and playing at the sleeping site before the real work of the day, finding food, has to begin. Such leisurely mornings tend to occur when food is most abundant. When food is hard to come by, baboons cannot afford such luxury and sometimes leave their sleeping sites before it is fully light in order to begin feeding. In the far south of Africa, which has a climate and seasons similar to those of Mediterranean Europe, it is just too cold to hang around on winter mornings. The baboons have to get moving quickly in order to get their blood pumping and their temperature up.

This is not a problem for the yellow baboons, though, who live in the tropical savannas of Kenya and Tanzania. For them, the morning social period comes to an end gradually as one or two of the adult baboons leave the sleeping site and move away to feed. Slowly, all the other baboons begin to follow. In areas where there are dangerous predators, it is important for the members of the group not to get separated from each other and, thus, place themselves in danger. As the baboons move out from the sleeping site, they either begin foraging immediately on whatever they happen to find as they wander along, or march off in a determined manner toward a particularly good area and begin the day's foraging there. Unlike most other African monkeys, baboons spend their waking hours almost exclusively on the ground, only occasionally climbing trees in order to feed on fruits or acacia pods.

By mid morning, most of the group will be feeding. The only exceptions are the young juvenile baboons, who often break off from foraging to

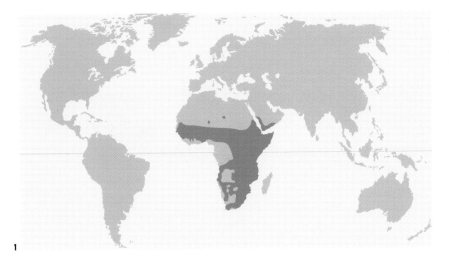

1. Baboons are the most widely distributed of all the African monkeys. They are found in virtually all parts of sub-Saharan Africa.

1

continue with the games they started at the sleeping site. If there are fertile females in the group, the adult males may also have trouble concentrating on their food. When female baboons are ready to mate, their bottoms swell up and are bright pink in color. When males see a female in this state, they attempt to mate with her as often as possible. They try to keep track of her movements and outmanouver all the other males in the group to stop them getting too close. Their eating habits suffer as a result and males may spend up to 20 percent less time feeding than usual when they are consorting in this way. On the other hand, females with young babies try not to be distracted from the serious business of eating. Producing milk to feed their infants is onerous, and females have to increase their feeding time by up to 75 percent to keep up with their infants' needs. As the mother

1

feeds, the infant clings to her chest and suckles with an intensity that matches her feeding efforts. Older infants ride on their mothers' backs, jockey style.

As the group moves along, the baboons keep in contact with each other by grunting softly. Sometimes an individual gets separated from the group and makes a "lost call," a short, sharp yelp, that reflects the animal's distress at finding itself alone. On other occasions, another baboon group may be spotted in the distance and the intensity of grunting increases to a frantic pitch.
If the other group approaches too close, the adult males in the troop may begin to make loud barking calls, known as "wa-hoos," and begin herding the females back to keep them out of contact with the males from the other troop. Spotting another group like this often results in a change of route so that the two groups do not make contact. When

changing direction, the baboons often increase the rate of contact grunting, and this may help the group stick together as they move on to an alternative path.

As midday approaches, and the sun reaches its zenith, it becomes intolerably hot. Unable to stay in the open and feed, the baboons retire to a shady grove of acacia trees and rest until the sun loses some of its heat. When things have cooled down, the baboons will once again begin foraging, gradually moving back toward the sleeping site they left that morning, or perhaps heading toward a different one if that is closer.

If food has been hard to come by that day, the baboons may remain feeding until the sun has almost set before climbing up into their sleeping trees and settling down. When conditions are cold and rainy, baboon groups may tailor their daily

1. Baboons are highly social monkeys. They can live in groups containing more than 100 animals.

 VOTING BABOONS

Each morning, the hamadryas baboons of northeast Africa vote on where they should go that day. Two or three males move to the periphery of the group and sit facing in a particular direction. The other males then express their preference by lining up behind one of these males. Males also engage in a behavior called "notifying". One runs up to another, stops short, peers into the other's face, then turns around, and presents his rear. It seems that the notifying male is informing others about his preference for a departure direction. Once a majority vote is reached, everyone sets off for the day's foraging.

movements so that they end up at a suitable site for sleeping. If life has been relatively easy, the baboons will gather around the sleeping site and once again engage in a relaxing grooming session. Some of the juveniles may still have enough energy left to play, but this is the time of day when most of them are happy to sit quietly and let their mothers, aunts, or grandmothers groom them. As darkness falls, the baboons begin to move up into the trees or onto the cliff that will be their resting place for the night. Some continue to groom even after it is too dark to see anymore. The soft grunting continues for a while as everyone settles down and finds a place to spend the night. The baboon day is at an end.

1

2

1. There is safety in numbers. These chacma baboons are crossing a swamp together in the Okavango Delta, in Botswana.

2. Yellow baboons feed and rest in a dry river bed. Most baboons retire to the shade during the hottest part of the day.

▶ A SAFE PLACE TO SNOOZE

Safety is a priority when choosing a sleeping site. Baboons cannot see well in the dark and they need to make sure that nocturnal predators, such as leopards, cannot launch a surprise attack. So baboons sleep in trees, or on high rocky cliffs, and they stick close together. A good sleeping site should also be dry and warm because temperatures can drop at night. A sheltered site can help baboons retain body heat and save precious energy. Most baboons use the same sites repeatedly and, in some areas, there are so few suitable sites that several groups are forced to sleep together.

THE CONQUERORS OF AFRICA

Baboons are large, sturdy monkeys. Adult males weigh between 22 to 30 kg on average, while adult females weigh between 12 to 15 kg. However, the hamadryas baboon of Ethiopia and Arabia is much smaller. Adult males weigh only 17 kg and adult females only 9 to 10 kg. Even so, hamadryas are still large for monkeys. Most tree-living species weigh only 6 to 10 kg. Baboons spend most of their time on the ground and it has been suggested that their large size helps protect them from predators. Leopards and lions are the only real threat to an adult baboon's safety, though infant baboons are also vulnerable to attack by large birds of prey, and in areas where chimpanzees and baboons are found together, chimpanzees occasionally hunt baboons. Living on the ground means that the baboon's hands and feet have become adapted to walking flat on the ground, rather than grasping

1. These guinea baboons from West Africa have a reddish-colored coat in contrast to the gray-brown of the other savanna baboons.

2. The gelada baboon from Ethiopia has a bare patch of red skin on its chest. This has led to the species being called the "bleeding heart" baboon.

branches in the tree tops. Their arms and legs are roughly equal in length, whereas tree-living monkeys have legs that are much longer than their arms, since this helps with balance high up in the canopy. Baboons do not need to worry about their balance, but they do need to scan the ground for danger. The length of their arms allows baboons to keep an eye out for any predators without having to crane their necks. Despite this redesign for life on the ground, they can climb trees, although adults often look clumsy because of their large bulk. The gelada baboon of Ethiopia is an exception. It has become so well adapted for life on the ground that it is not good at climbing.

Baboons are doglike in appearance, with a large protruding muzzle. Their ears are small and lie flat to the head. Adult males have a more well-defined muzzle than the females, and there are extra bony ridges along the sides of the nose. Males also have large, sharp canine teeth, which are twice the size of females' teeth. They keep these canine teeth razor sharp by grinding them against a specially adapted tooth in the lower jaw. The sound of a male grinding his teeth is a good indicator that fighting is likely to break out.

Baboons have small close-set eyes and extremely sharp vision. They often spot things in the distance long before a human observer can see what they are looking at. Vision is the baboons' primary sense, and they have a large variety of facial expressions that they use to convey threats, submission, and friendly overtures to another animal. They also have a wide array of vocalizations.

2

Baboons have specially adapted sitting pads on their bottoms which allow them to sit comfortably on hard surfaces.

Baboons are gray-brown in color, although the exact shade varies according to where in Africa they are found. The fur covering their bodies is short and much finer on the chest and stomach. The skin shows through in these areas, and may have a bluish cast. Male baboons often have impressive capes and manes of hair on their head and shoulders which make them look bigger and intimidate their rivals in fights. Baboons have short tails compared to forest monkeys, and the first third of the tail is rigid and sticks straight up from the back. Infants sometimes use this as a back rest when riding on their mothers' back. Tail length and shape are variable between animals and it is possible to tell individual baboons apart by features of their tails alone.

Adult baboons walk in a measured and dignified way, and are much less flighty and twitchy than the smaller monkey species. Youngsters, on the other hand, charge around in an energetic fashion, investigating and poking their noses into everything they come across. Although they can appear calm, baboons are excitable animals. Squabbles and fights break out at the slightest

PRIMATE CLASSIFICATION: BABOONS

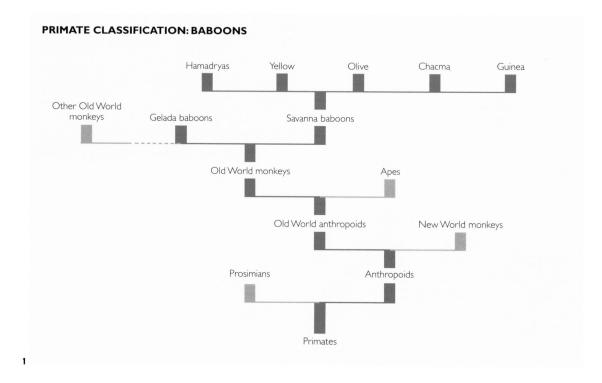

1

excuse and are accompanied by loud screams and other vocalizations. It is common to hear a baboon group approaching before it comes into view.

Baboons are inquisitive and smart. They are always investigating new things they come across in the environment, although youngsters and adult males are more adventurous than adult females, who tend to be more conservative.

Baboon species

Baboons are the most successful of all the African monkeys. They are found from the plateaus of the Ethiopian highlands in the north to the coastal scrub of the Cape of Good Hope in the far south, from the humid woodlands of Senegal in the west to the vast savannas of Kenya and Tanzania in the east. There is even a population of hamadryas baboons across the Red Sea in Arabia. It is unclear whether they made it there on their own, via a bridge of land that has now submerged beneath the sea, or whether they were taken there by humans. Baboons are found in deserts, rain forests, and mountain ranges.

Baboons can be grouped into two genera, each genus containing just one living species, the *Theropithecus* baboons, of which the gelada baboon is the only living species, and the *Papio* or "savanna" baboons. Due to differences in appearance, the savanna baboons were initially placed into five separate species, but since all *Papio* species can, and do, interbreed, it became more common to consider them as a single species, *Papio cynocephalus*, divided into five subspecies:

2

1. The baboons are descendants of the Old World monkeys. There are two genera, gelada baboons and the savanna baboons, which are further divided into five subspecies.

2. Baboons can find food to eat almost anywhere, both above and below ground. This young chacma baboon gnaws on the fruit of the "sausage tree" (*Kigelia africana*).

yellow (*Papio cynocephalus cynocephalus*), olive (*Papio cynocephalus anubis*), guinea (*Papio cynocephalus papio*), chacma (*Papio cynocephalus ursinus*), and hamadryas baboons (*Papio cynocephalus hamadryas*).

Hamadryas baboons are the most different from the other baboons in both their appearance and their behavior. They are the most northerly of the five subspecies found in the arid scrublands and deserts of Ethiopia, Sudan, Somalia, and on the coast of southern Arabia. Their distribution grades into that of olive baboons, which range from Ethiopia through to northern Tanzania and across to West Africa. The yellow baboons are found from Tanzania through to Zambia and northern Mozambique and across to Angola, while the chacma baboons are found throughout southern Africa, from the middle of Zambia to the Cape Province of South Africa. The guinea baboon has a restricted distribution in West Africa. The gelada species also has a restricted distribution and is found only in the highlands of the Simen Mountains in Ethiopia. The guinea baboons have a reddish-colored coat, while the olive baboons have a thick greenish-gray coat. Olive baboons are also

 NOT SO CLOSE RELATIVES . . .

Mandrills and drills are large, ground-living monkeys that inhabit the tropical forests of West Africa. Both species look like baboons. They are large and stocky, with dog-like muzzles and similar body proportions, but unlike baboons they have short tails. Due to these similarities in appearance, mandrills and drills were traditionally considered to be a species of baboon. However, recent molecular studies of blood proteins and DNA have revealed that they are actually not baboons at all, and are more closely related to another species of forest monkey, the terrestrial mangabeys (*Cercocebus*).

a

b

1

robust and stocky compared to the other types of baboon, and they have an overhanging tip to their nose. Adult male olive baboons also have a large furry mane.

Yellow baboons have a yellow coat and they are slender, with long legs, and they have an up-turned nose. Again, the males have a mane of furry hair around their heads. The chacma baboons of southern Africa are dark in color and have a furry fringe of black hair around their neck and shoulders. The males also have a cape of hair across their shoulders. The hamadryas differs in appearance from the other savanna baboons. It is much smaller, with a light gray coat and a pink face and bottom. Males are much larger than females and have a mane of longer hair around their head and shoulders.

Gelada baboon males also have a mane, though it is longer, silkier, and much more magnificent than that of the male hamadryas baboon. Both male and female gelada baboons have patches of bare skin on their chests. These are bright red in color and have earned the gelada the name of the "bleeding heart" baboon.

Hybrid baboons are fertile and can breed,

1. The five subspecies of *Papio,* or "savanna" baboons: (a) hamadryas, (b) olive, (c) guinea, (d) chacma, (e) yellow. The gelada (f) is the only living species of *Theropithecus* baboon.

HOME RANGES IN DIFFERENT HABITATS

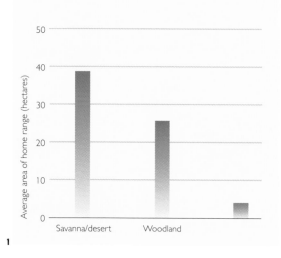

1

HUNTING IN DIFFERENT HABITATS

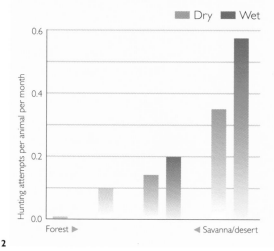

2

1, 2. In poor habitats, where vegetation is scarce, baboons increase the area of their home range and the amount of meat they eat.

3. Baboons are fond of fruit. It makes a convenient snack. Most other baboon foods require a lot more effort to find and eat.

indicating that the differences between baboons is superficial, genetically speaking. Some other mammals are able to mate with each other and produce offspring; horses and donkeys, for example, can mate and produce mules, but these offspring are sterile because the genetic differences between the parent species are too large to allow the production of fertile eggs and sperm. The fact that different types of baboon can interbreed and produce fertile offspring suggests that, despite their differences, they are really all members of the same species. Although enough time has passed to produce differences in appearance and behavior, there has not been any major genetic overhaul. Under their skin, baboons are all the same.

A VARIED DIET

Baboons are hardy animals. They can withstand extreme temperatures and rainfall and "tough it out" in the most remarkable fashion. This ability to cope with almost anything that nature throws at them partly explains why baboons are so successful as a species. The other key to their success is their ability to eat almost anything. The diet of most baboons is astonishingly diverse. They eat fruit, leaves, seeds, grass, berries, flowers, roots, shoots, gum, insects, and even meat. This is not to say that they are not discerning, however. Although baboons will eat practically anything they come across in their natural habitat, they often eat only one particular part of any food. They may eat only the leaf petioles, the tender nodule where a leaf joins a stem, of one species, or only the flower buds of another. They may spend five minutes or so digging up an enormous sedge plant, only to nibble briefly and delicately at its roots. This combination of diversity and discernment is highly characteristic of baboons, as is their ability to exploit foods found below, as well as above, ground.

Because baboons' hands are like human hands and they are capable of gripping fine objects between the thumb and forefinger, they can pluck individual grass blades and flowers and strip open seed pods. They are also able to pick up small seeds, some no larger than an apple pit, from the ground. They do all this at a rapid pace and can eat large numbers of these items in a short space of time. During a study of the chacma baboons in the Drakensberg Mountains in South Africa,

3

Baboons that live in the Namib Desert in southern Africa can go for 100 days without water.

primatologist Andrew Whiten once calculated that a group of five baboons had consumed more than 30,000 Morea flowers in the space of only two-and-a-half hours. This ability to manipulate things with their hands and fingers is one of the reasons why baboons were able to colonize the savannas so successfully. Unlike the forests where most monkeys live, food does not always grow on trees in the tropical grasslands. Baboons are able to cope with those times of the year when food is scarce by harvesting the resources that are abundant below ground. The hamadryas baboons of Ethiopia and the mountain chacma baboons of South Africa are entirely dependent on items such as roots, bulbs, and corms during certain periods of the year. Without the ability to make use of these resources with their manipulation skills, the baboons would be unable to survive.

Food-gathering techniques

Baboons are adept at spotting clues that tell them that a tasty corm or bulb is lurking underground. Often this clue is nothing more than a small shoot poking up from the ground. A baboon will begin scratching at the dirt around the shoot with its forefinger. Once it has made a small hole, it will start digging more enthusiastically, using both hands, like a dog digging for a bone. When the hole is deep enough, the baboon will wiggle the corm out of the surrounding dirt, again using its forefinger, and then clean any excess dirt and grit from it by rubbing it up and down its arm in a sweeping motion.

Baboons also dig up ants' nests in a similar way. They extract the nest, and its heaving mass of soldier and worker ants, and then rapidly lick and

▶ SOME LIKE IT HOT …

Baboons are able to cope with extreme conditions. Those of the Namib Desert, for example, have to cope with temperatures in excess of 40°C. Baboons use various behavioral tactics to avoid the worst effects of the weather. In most areas of Africa, they take time out from their foraging midday and rest quietly in the shade. In more southerly habitats, keeping the cold out can also be a problem. During the winter, baboons in the Cape Province of South Africa seek the most sheltered areas of their home range and use the most secluded sleeping sites to help conserve their energy on cold, windy days.

1. (opposite) Baboons have strong jaws and teeth and can make short work of the thick rinds and protective casings around fruits.

1. Baboons obtain much of their food from underground and sometimes even underwater. This chacma baboon is foraging for water lily tubers.

2. Baboons are fond of meat. Hunting is rare, however, and tends to occur in harsh habitats when other food is scarce.

bite off as many as possible. They have to be quick, because the ants swarm off the nest and onto the baboons' bodies. Once they have worked their way through the thick fur, they give painful bites. Honey is another prized baboon food, and baboons seem attuned to the location of bees' nests. When they encounter bees flying around in a particular area, they will begin searching for a nest in any likely hole in the ground.

Baboons are also fond of fruit. One favorite of the olive baboon is the prickly pear, which is covered with small, irritating hairs that protect the fruit and stop it being eaten. The hairs are no defense against baboons, however, They knock the fruit from the plant, and then roll it around in the dirt before eating it to remove all the hairs that could irritate the mouth and throat. Chacma baboons living in a woodland habitat in Zululand, South Africa, also make the most of the fruits in their habitat. Some even provide two chances to make a tasty feast. During the fruiting season of the marula tree, baboons climb up and feed on the sweet flesh of the fruits. They discard the nuts and drop them to the ground, where they join those that have fallen from the tree naturally. After a month or two of drying out on the ground, the baboons return to eat the insides of the hard nuts. They crack them open with their teeth, and then pull out the inside of the nut with their fingers or hook it out using one of their canine teeth.

Meat eating

It is in harsh habitats, when other foods are in short supply, that meat eating is most common. Hunting for meat is time-consuming and costly in energy, so it is only used as a last resort when baboons cannot get all that they need from plant resources.

All baboons eat animal matter of some sort or another – insects, larvae, and grubs, plus the occasional bird's egg. In some areas, however, baboons have been found to eat meat. This is usually small infant antelope that they find hidden in the grass, or baby ostriches that have become separated from their mothers.

Another meaty food that baboons appear able to exploit is the tortoise. In the western Cape, chacma baboons have been observed to eat tortoises as though they were small meat pies wrapped in a particularly tough pastry case. Only small tortoises are eaten, probably because the shell is much thinner and easier to crack.

When a baboon comes across a tortoise of the right size, it picks it up and, with the head-end facing the baboon, wedges the underside of the carapace under its incisor teeth. The tortoise retreats inside its shell as soon as the baboon touches it, so this is an easy operation to achieve. Once the tortoise is wedged in the right position, the baboon pulls hard at the carapace with enough force to crack it open. It then feeds on the tortoise meat inside.

Although larger tortoises are not actually eaten, it is common to come across tortoises lying on their backs, with gnaw marks on their carapaces, suggesting that a baboon has made an unsuccessful attempt to get inside.

2

☆ Baboons can store food in special cheek pouches that lie just under the skin on either side of the jaw. They push food into the pouches through small slits on the insides of their cheeks and can then eat it later.

A grassy diet

The gelada baboon of Ethiopia is the one exception to the pattern of wide-ranging dietary tastes. It lives on only one type of food: grass. To be fair, it does eat a wide range of different grass species, and it eats practically every bit of a grass plant, from seeds to rhizomes (fine root-like structures). Nevertheless, the gelada diet is boring by baboon standards. Not that gelada have much choice: their mountainous home is at too high an altitude for most kinds of trees to grow, so fruit is not really an option, and the diversity of plant species in these highland grasslands is rather paltry compared to those that grow lower down.

The gelada, however, seem perfectly happy and are well adapted to their grassy diet. They are the most dextrous of all the baboon species, with a fine precision grip that allows them to pluck individual grass blades quickly and efficiently.

Gelada baboons sit on their bottoms and harvest the patch of grass immediately in front of them. When they have eaten all that is within their reach, instead of getting up and walking on to a fresh patch of grass like any other baboon would do, they shuffle along on their bottoms, continuing to harvest handfuls as they go. This 'shuffle-walking' is a distinctive gelada behavior that is used for gathering food such as grass, which is widely and evenly distributed.

1

1. An infant baboon sits surrounded by blossoms. The flowers are ideal food for young baboons and are easy to pick.

2. A baboon gnaws on the gum produced under the bark of a tree. Gum contains valuable nutrients and also provides some liquid for baboons when water is scarce.

Thriving populations

Baboons are able to find food practically anywhere: their inquisitiveness means they are willing to investigate any possible food source, while their intelligence and ability to manipulate objects allows them to extract food, no matter how well protected or well hidden it is. They are extremely resourceful when it comes to getting into somewhere they shouldn't, frequently raiding crop fields and tourist camps. Understandably, this makes them rather unpopular and they are officially declared as vermin in many parts of Africa – a designation that reflects their ability to thrive in human habitats. In tourist areas, however, humans are at least partly to blame for the baboons' bad reputation. A baboon that feeds on the crumbs offered by a visitor is considered cute; but the same baboon loses its appeal rapidly when, in search of more tasty morsels, it turns the campsite upside-down while the owners are away, or aggressively snatches food from them. A baboon has to spend practically all day feeding in its usual habitat to take in as many calories as there are in a single slice of bread. It is no wonder that, once they have got a taste for it, baboons will stop at nothing to steal human food. The only way to stop baboons becoming a tourist problem is to ensure people resist the temptation to feed them in the first place. If baboons do not associate humans with food, then they will not bother humans for it.

One positive aspect of the baboons' ability to thrive in human habitats is the fact that, unlike the populations of most other large African mammals,

2

baboon populations are thriving and they are not an endangered species. But we should not be too complacent about the baboons' success. Humans often attempt to eradicate baboons because they are pests, and where this becomes excessive, baboon populations can become endangered just like any other species. The baboon population of Cape Point, South Africa, is one example of how this has happened. So many baboons have been shot as pests that the population is now too small to remain viable. It is likely to become extinct there in the next few years unless drastic remedial action is taken to preserve those that remain.

SOCIAL LIFE

SOCIAL LIFE

Monkeys are the most sociable of all the primates, and baboons are among the most sociable of all monkeys. Females form the core of baboon society. In all species, except for the unusual hamadryas, females never leave the group that they are born into. They grow up surrounded by their relatives, forming close relationships that last a lifetime. Although males are larger and more powerful than females, their role is more peripheral. They may stay only a few years in any particular group before moving off to make another life for themselves elsewhere.

Understanding the social life of baboons means understanding the way that animals form and maintain relationships with each other, how they learn whom to groom, whom to submit to, and whom to dominate. It also means looking at baboons as individuals. No two baboons are the same, and their behavior reflects their unique experiences within the group.

Previous page: A chacma baboon grooms a young one with its tongue. Grooming is more usually performed with the hands among baboons.

BABOON GROUPS

Within a baboon group, the females with young infants tend to occupy the most central positions. This is partly intentional, because central positions are safer, but mothers also tend to be surrounded by lots of other animals who wish to interact with their babies. Pregnant females, on the other hand, often stick to the edge of the group, where they are less likely to be disturbed. They need to concentrate on feeding in readiness for the birth of their infant, and they may also want to avoid aggression since they are heavy and unable to move quickly.

During the early days of baboon studies, adult males were thought to occupy positions from which they could protect the females and infants in the group. However, this is a fallacy they are often the first to run at any sign of trouble. Adult males can also be peripheral. Many males will wander far away from the group on their own to feed, often leaving the sleeping site before any other animals in order to do so. Their tendency to do this depends on how dangerous the environment is. In areas of high predator risk, males tend to stick with the troop more closely. Males also become more central when they are courting fertile females. They stick close by the females that they are interested in to protect their mating rights, drawing them into a more central position.

Young infants stay close to their mothers, but older infants and juveniles form playgroups of their own and can often be far away from their mothers. Groups of juveniles also forage together, seeming to get a lot of information about what foods are good to eat from their peers. In addition, these "bratpacks" are often attracted to the dominant adult male in

1. A group of olive baboon females and their young. Females form the core of baboon society and remain in the same group for their entire lives.

1

the group. They will follow him around in a group, feeding on the scraps he leaves behind and watching his activities with interest.

Groups of yellow, olive, and chacma baboons range in size from 20 to 150 animals, though the average is 40 to 80. In a group of this size, there will usually be 10 to 12 adult females and 2 to 5 adult males, with the remainder being infants and juveniles of various ages. Depending on its size, a group will move 1 to 5 km per day. The bigger the group, the longer the day's journey. When food is scarce, groups can range up to 9 to 10 km per day, although this is rare.

Living with relatives

Within groups of yellow, chacma, and olive baboons, females form the core of baboon society. This means that all females in a baboon group are related to each other in some way. Baboon groups are made up of one large extended family of females, and a female baboon grows up surrounded by her mother, sisters, aunts, and cousins. These female families are known as matrilines. Baboon females can also be related through their father's line. Since the dominant male in a baboon group usually gets the most matings, he fathers most of the offspring born during a particular period. This means that two females from completely different matrilines, and often at opposite ends of the dominance hierarchy, may actually be as closely related to each other as they are to the half sisters they share on their mother's side. Female baboons have no way of knowing that they are related in this way and it does not seem to influence the way dominant females treat subordinates who could be their half sisters.

Females live with their relatives because it is the easiest way to form groups. Social groups did not come out of nowhere during the course of evolution. They had to be built one step at a time. The simplest way to form a social group from a solitary-living animal is for offspring to remain with their mother at adulthood, rather than leaving to go off alone. Living in a group also requires a certain amount of trust, and females are able to make more accurate assessments of the reliability of their close relatives than they are of strangers. Growing up together gives females plenty of opportunity to witness another female's reliability as a result of her own experience and those of others. As a result, their trust is less likely to be abused. Living with relatives therefore makes sense for female baboons.

The fact that females remain in the same group throughout their lives has repercussions for the males born into a group. Mating with relatives is usually avoided because of the risk of producing poor-quality offspring through inbreeding. While a male lives with his mother, sisters, aunts, and cousins, his mating options are limited. As a result, male baboons do not have any other choice than to

2

1. Chacma baboons forage in the late afternoon. A group is usually well coordinated; animals stick together in case of predator attack.

2. Female baboons and their infants live with their close relatives. The females form close bonds with each other.

Gelada females have a number of small white blisters on their chest, which swell up when they are fertile and ready to mate.

leave the groups they are born into and seek out others where they are unrelated to the females. However, this initial move does not completely solve the problem for males. After a few years in the new troop, a male will have fathered a number of offspring, some of whom will be female. When these females reach adulthood, a male risks mating with his own daughter and faces a similar problem of inbreeding that he had in his original group. Consequently, males continue to move from troop to troop throughout their lives.

Guinea baboons

Although much is known about the yellow, olive, and chacma baboons, the social organization of the guinea baboon is more of a mystery. This is mainly because it lives in the humid grasslands of West Africa, where the grass may grow as high as 4 m.

It is difficult to follow and observe baboons under these conditions, and there has only ever been one detailed study of the guinea baboons' behavior. Although the basic social structure of guinea baboon groups is the same as that of the other savanna baboons, they tend to live in much larger groups. These groups can sometimes contain as many as 200 animals. Guinea baboons have to live in large groups because poor visibility in their dense savanna woodland habitat means that the risk of surprise by a predator is high. The more eyes and ears available to detect danger, the less likely an attack. Finding food for all members of these large groups is not a problem because guinea baboons live in habitats containing high-quality food resources. However, guinea baboon groups are much less stable than other savanna baboon groups. During the course of a day's foraging they break up into smaller groups, which consist of a

1. (opposite) A female hamadryas inspects her newborn infant. The bonds formed between mothers and offspring are strong.

▷ WA-HOOS AND GRUNTS

Baboons are noisy monkeys. One of the most distinctive vocalizations is the males' loud barking call, known as the "wa-hoo." Males often produce wa-hoos during encounters with strange baboon groups, during aggressive incidents with other males in their own troop, or when they get separated from the rest of the troop. Females and young animals make a noise like a yelp when they find themselves alone. Baboons also grunt softly to each other when grooming, and often greet and inspect new mothers and their infants using a distinctive grunting sound.

male, two or three females, and their young. Again, poor visibility seems to be the cause. As the group spreads out to forage they cannot remain coordinated in the dense undergrowth. The subgroups manage to keep in contact, however, and track each others' movements by means of loud calls produced by the adult males. At the end of the day, the entire group joins up again as they approach their sleeping site.

Harems and clans

Generally speaking, chacma, olive, yellow and guinea baboon groups are not highly structured. Each baboon tends to do its own thing, although activities are more or less coordinated so that all of them stay together and out of danger.

The same is not true of the hamadryas and gelada baboons, who live in societies that are much more complex and multi-layered. Their basic social unit consists of a harem, a single male plus a number of females and their associated offspring. In the hamadryas baboons, two or three harems will join together to form a clan. The male members of a clan are all related to each other and are usually brothers. A number of these clans join together to form a band containing about 60 animals. In some areas, a lack of suitable sleeping sites means that several bands may converge on a single tree or cliff to form a large "sleeping troop."

Gelada baboons also form bands containing between two and 25 harems. These bands then join together during the day into a large foraging herd that may contain as many as 600 animals. Large herds are a defense against predators in the open habitats of the Ethiopian highlands where geladas

Previous page:
Juvenile baboons settle down for the night. When they are young, baboons sleep near their mothers. As they grow, they prefer to be near their playmates.

1

live. In both hamadryas and gelada, bands also contain adult males who do not have their own groups of females. In the gelada, these males form stable all-male groups.

While these grouping patterns may seem almost identical, males and females behave differently in the gelada and hamadryas species. In the gelada, the females in a harem are all closely related, and focus most of their social attention on each other. The male is a peripheral figure. Unlike the sociable females, gelada males rarely interact with each other and are wary about letting other males get too close to themselves or to their females. In contrast, male hamadryas are often seen interacting socially, and it is the females that tend not to socialize with each other. Hamadryas females within a harem are not closely related and prefer to spend their time grooming the harem male. The male keeps the

2

1. Gelada baboons can form enormous herds of up to 600 animals. Each herd consists of a number of harems, containing a single male, several females, and their associated offspring.

2. The hamadryas male lives in a small harem with a number of females. Several of these harems form a "clan." The males in each clan may be related to each other.

 SOCIAL STRESSES

Among gelada baboons, social factors play a role in the number of offspring females produce. Lower-ranking females tend to produce offspring at a much slower rate than higher-ranking females and also experience more threats and aggression. This increase in the level of stress hormones in the blood seems to stop the production of hormones that are essential for reproduction. Gelada females are not particularly aggressive. On average, a female will threaten another about once per day. However, even these low levels of aggression work, because the effect of these threats tends to add up considerably, especially further down the hierarchy where most aggression takes place. It takes a low-ranking female 4 to 5 months longer to conceive than it does a high-ranking female.

females close to him by aggressively herding them together, and often punishes a straying female by biting her on the neck, an act no gelada male would even dare contemplate.

These differences between the two species in grooming preferences and social tendencies become clear if the harem male dies or disappears. Among hamadryas baboons, females tend to disperse to other groups and the group falls apart completely without the male to hold it together. In the gelada, on the other hand, females seem scarcely to notice if the male is missing and they remain as a stable, solidly bonded group. Another male will then attach himself to the group as a whole. This difference

reults from the fact that gelada females are closely related to each other, while hamadryas females are not. The harsh habitat in which hamadryas live means that infant death rates are high and it takes females a long time to produce an offspring that will survive until adulthood. Therefore female hamadryas grow up in small kin groups, usually just the daughter and her mother. Females get separated from their mothers when an adult male hamadryas kidnaps them for his breeding unit. The lack of kin support means that hamadryas males can exert more control over females than gelada baboons, leading to an entirely different social structure.

1

2

SOCIAL RELATIONSHIPS

Baboons are highly sociable animals and spend a lot of time engaged in one social behavior in particular: grooming. When one animal grooms another, it searches carefully through its partner's fur, pulling off ticks, dead skin, and other parasites. In most cases, baboons groom those areas that an animal cannot see or reach on its own, such as the back and the top of the head. When baboons want to be groomed, they will approach their chosen partner and present their shoulder or their flank to the other animal. If the other animal is willing to participate, it will begin grooming. If it is not so willing, it will ignore the other baboon's request. When this happens, the presenting baboon may leave and try to find another partner, or it may begin grooming the other animal itself, possibly with the hope that its efforts will be reciprocated. When adult males want to be groomed by a female, they present themselves by flopping down in front of them in an unceremonious fashion. Usually, the female will comply. If she does not and attempts to leave the male, he will often chase and attack her until she gives in and grooms him.

Juvenile baboons forego any formalities when they groom each other. They simply march up to the animal of their choice, grab hold of it, and begin grooming. Infants who are less than six months old rarely groom any other animals, and are groomed mainly by their mothers. Once they reach six months of age, they begin to groom their mothers. By 12 months, they will have started to groom other infants and juveniles. Over the next few years,

1. A male gelada baboon with his harem of females. Gelada females prefer their own company to that of the male.

2. The protection provided by living in a group is important for females with young infants.

 Female baboons usually give birth at night. During the day there is a risk of getting left behind by the rest of the troop, and a female is more vulnerable to predators.

they gradually increase the amount of time spent grooming adult females. In the case of young females, this helps them integrate themselves into the adult social network.

The function of grooming

Baboons sometimes spend up to two hours a day grooming each other. A typical baboon day begins and ends with a lengthy grooming session, and they usually squeeze in one or two more if they get the chance. Clearly, grooming is an important activity for baboons, but what exactly do they get out of it? One of the major reasons for animals to groom is to keep clean and tick free, since this helps reduce the chance of contracting disease.

However, baboons spend more time grooming than is necessary for keeping clean. This may be because grooming is an enjoyable experience for a baboon. Animals become visibly more relaxed over

1. Unlike most baboons, female hamadryas prefer to groom the harem male rather than groom the other females living in the harem.

2. Grooming is usually done to the exclusion of all other activities, but here a young baboon combines business with pleasure and continues to forage during grooming.

 THE GROOMING TRADE

Baboon groups can be compared to market places where individuals trade for what they need. Baboons trade grooming in return for more grooming, but they also trade it for other things. Females will trade grooming in return for being tolerated around a new baby. When lower-ranking females want to handle the infants of higher-ranking females, the amount of time they have to spend grooming is much higher than that paid by females who are more similar in rank to the mother. Male baboons use grooming to buy a female's loyalty.

the course of a grooming session and may often fall asleep. All the pulling and tugging of an animal's fur leads to the release of chemicals in the brain known as beta-endorphins. These chemicals are similar to opium-like drugs and they produce a feeling of wellbeing and relaxation. It seems that baboons are addicted to grooming because of the pleasant sensations that it produces. The production of beta-endorphins means that grooming is an ideal behavior for keeping the peace in a baboon troop. Whenever things get tense, or when actual aggression breaks out, grooming is used to restore calm between the fighting animals. Fighting is common in baboon troops. Although females live with their relatives, this does not necessarily mean that relationships are cordial.

2

1

1. Grooming is so pleasurable and relaxing that baboons often nod off during the course of a lengthy session.

2. Baboons usually groom each other in the places that are hard to reach, such as the back of the head.

When fights break out, grooming is often used to signal an end to hostilities and it also reduces the chance that the former opponents will continue to behave aggressively toward each other.

Dominance in females

Living in a group automatically increases the competition for food. Within baboon groups, females use their relationships with other animals to try to reduce the effects of this competition. Establishing dominance over another animal is the most straightforward way for individuals to ensure they get their hands on scarce food resources. Dominant females are often larger than sub-ordinate females and they may also be more aggressive. They are able to monopolize food and prevent the lower-ranking animals from getting it. Low-ranking females have their own tactics to circumvent these problems. One way is to ingratiate oneself with dominant animals by grooming them. This can increase the likelihood that the dominant one will tolerate a subordinate at a feeding site, and allow the lower-ranking animal to gain access. Lower-ranking females may also gang up on a dominant individual, using force to gain access to food. However, this behavior is found only among the East African baboons, and does not occur at all in the chacma baboons of southern Africa.

Among female baboons, dominant relationships tend to be strict. Each female can be ranked in the hierarchy and these ranks remain stable over a long period of time. Once dominance is established, females usually maintain their position. They need only threaten subordinate females, rather than launch an all-out attack, and they do not have to do this often. Some researchers say that baboons have a subordinant, rather than a dominant, hierarchy

1. Young baboons will often follow an older animal around while it forages. They take advantage of food scraps and learn what is good to eat.

2. A baboon "presents" to another. This is a submissive gesture performed by subordinates toward more dominant animals.

2

because it is the actions of the lower-ranking animals that seem to maintain the status quo.

When a dominant female approaches, low-ranking females will present their rear ends to her, acknowledging that she is dominant to them. If she is dominant, they may cringe or cower and grimace in fear. Dominant females sometimes reassure low-ranking females by briefly touching their sides and lipsmacking or grunting at them.

Sex and rank

In baboon groups, females belonging to the same family have similar dominance ranks. Females have to push their way into the established adult hierarchy, and they rely on the backing of their relatives to help them. However, this only happens as they approach adulthood. Juvenile baboon females play with each other and with young infant baboons without any regard for rank or dominance.

As they approach sexual maturity, the young females begin to challenge adult females and behave aggressively toward them. They tend to direct these attacks at females who are lower-ranking than their own adult female relatives. Their adult kin support them in their attempts at social-climbing, ensuring that lower-ranking females submit to these young upstarts. Young females do not behave aggressively to females who are higher ranking than their relatives because, even with their relatives' support, they cannot force the dominant female to submit.

These young females are eventually able to dominate lower-ranking females without any aid from their relatives, at which point they become fully integrated members of the adult female hierarchy. As they are able to dominate those females who rank below their relatives but remain subordinate to those who dominate their relatives, they occupy a position in the hierarchy that is adjacent to their female kin.

Dominance in males

Males also show dominant relationships, although these tend to be more unstable than those among females. In yellow and olive baboons, the dominant rank a male occupies depends on his age, the amount of time he has been in a group, and whether he is an immigrant male or one who was born in the troop. When a male enters a group, he often behaves aggressively and assumes top, or alpha, status quickly. During this period, he frequently achieves high mating success with females. However, after he has been in the troop for a while he inevitably begins to face challenges from new males who arrived after him. A male may drop in rank as a consequence of the challenge so that long-term residents often hold lower ranks than males who have just arrived. However, males can prevent a drop in rank by forming coalitions with other males. A coalition is formed when two males gang up together and fight a third, more dominant, male. Their combined power allows them to defeat a male whom they would be unable to defeat alone. These coalitions are usually formed over access to fertile females. Males use coalitions to break up a relationship between a male and a female and one of the fighting males then takes over.

The frequent movement of males in and out of troops, in combination with coalition formation, means that males do not form stable dominance hierarchies. A male's rank can change on an almost weekly basis, depending on whether he can find a coalition partner, whether or not a new male has entered the group or an old one has left, or even if he has been injured in a fight or is just a bit under the weather due to illness. Although the dominance hierarchy as a whole may be unstable, it is always possible to identify the male who is currently top ranking or alpha at any one time, as all other males will defer to him.

▷ REPRODUCTIVE SUCCESS

It is easy to spot the alpha male in savanna baboon troop. He always has more of a swagger. Dominant (alpha) males are usually the most successful at mating. When a female is at the peak of fertility, the alpha male forms a "consortship" with her and prevents all the other males from mating, which helps ensure that he fertilizes the female and fathers her offspring. However, things do not always go smoothly. If the group is large, there may be several females ready to mate at the same time. The alpha male cannot monopolize all of them, and then has no choice but to allow lower-ranking males to mate too. Sometimes, lower-ranking males form co-operative coalitions to help them get a chance to mate. The males may harass the consorting male until he leaves the female to chase and fight with one of them. At this point, the other coaltion male seizes his opportunity and mates with the female.

SPECIAL FRIENDSHIPS

When male savanna baboons enter a new troop, the other animals are initially wary of the newcomer. The resident males treat the new male cautiously because they have no idea exactly how strong he is, and whether or not he could defeat them in a fight. Although they appear to ignore him, they are usually watching him closely. Females are also reluctant to get too close. As the reason that males enter a new troop is to increase their chance of mating with females, this is rather unfortunate; but as befits animals as intelligent as baboons, males use their social skills to overcome these obstacles.

When he first arrives, a new male usually sits on the periphery of the group that he wishes to join. Although apparently foraging like everyone else, the male is usually paying close attention to what all the others are doing. This goes on for a few days as the male gradually familiarizes himself with the members of his chosen troop. Then he seems to come to a decision. He picks one particular female and sits close to her, but not too close to scare her into moving away. Again, the male is patient and waits as the female gets used to this new turn of events. After a while, the male will begin to solicit the female and try to get her to groom with him. After a few attempts, the male will usually succeed, and the two animals slowly build up a relationship. As the female becomes more familiar with the male, other females become more interested in her new friend, and the male gets a chance to interact with more members of the troop. Soon the male will have changed from being a solitary and

1. An adult male guinea baboon with two female admirers. Male and female baboons are most closely associated during a female's fertile period.

peripheral male to a fully integrated group member. By this time, the male will have developed relationships with other females, though the female he approached initially will always be his "special friend".

Such special friendships have been found in all the savanna baboon populations that have been studied. They can persist for many years, and males may also develop close relationships with the female's offspring. Males and females with a special friendship behave differently toward each other than they do toward other members of the troop. The male, in particular, is willing to spend much more time grooming the female, whereas with other females, the male is happy to let the female do all the grooming. There is also some suggestion that females prefer to mate with their special friends more than with any other male, and that they swap sex for the protection that the male provides for the female and her offspring, but this is not always the case.

Fighting it out

Not all male baboons form special friendships. In some cases, a new male will sweep into a troop and fight it out with the other males for the dominant position. He will then compete for mating with fertile females, but will otherwise show little interest in them. It has been suggested that in these cases, the males are young and powerful and willing to risk injury to get the top position, while special friendship males are older and looking for a less risky way to get into the group. Generally, this does seems to be the case, but not all young males go for the rather gung-ho dominance strategy. It seems that males assess how powerful they are

1

1. A group of baboons resting and socializing. Young animals like grooming and building up relationships with their group mates.

2. An adult male baboon inspects a young infant while its mother looks on. Male and female baboons sometimes form special friendships and spend a good deal of time in one another's company.

2

relative to the other males in the group and then make their decision accordingly.

Special friendships are found only in baboons that live in groups that include several males. Among the hamadryas and gelada, where animals live in one-male units, males and females tend not to form mutually supportive relationships, partly because males do not need to ingratiate themselves with females to the same extent. Hamadryas males control the much smaller females with aggression and punishment. A

gelada male tries to maintain cordial grooming relationships with all the females in his unit, but only rarely is a female interested in forming a relationship with him, preferring the company of females. If a male and a female gelada do form a close relationship, this is usually because the female does not have any close relatives that she can groom with and this is the next best thing that she can do. Unlike savanna baboon friend-ships, however, the female does most of the grooming required to maintain the relationship.

GROWING UP

3 | GROWING UP

Baboon infants take a long time to grow up. As well as growing physically, they need to learn all the various skills that are necessary to cope with the demands of baboon life. They must learn what to feed on and when, who to groom with, and who to avoid. They need to know how to attract the opposite sex and how to out-compete the opposition. These are not skills that can be acquired overnight. A long juvenile period gives young baboons plenty of time to learn and practice the skills they will need as adults.

The kinds of skills that youngsters learn depend on where they live, the type of group that they grow up in, the kind of mother they have, whether she is casual or over protective, and whether they are male or female. All these factors combine to produce a unique learning experience for each individual baboon, and one that influences the way it will treat its own offspring in the future.

Previous page: Young baboon infants spend a lot of time playing together. This helps them develop their social skills.

INFANT DEVELOPMENT

Baboon infants are well developed at birth. Their eyes are open, and they cling to their mother's body with a vice-like grip. They are covered in a fine, downy coat of black hair and they have bright pink faces and ears. For the first month or so of life, infant baboons do little apart from suckle and sleep, clinging tightly to their mother's chest. This is just as well, since they are uncoordinated and vulnerable. During these first few weeks of life, infants are a source of intense interest to other members of the group. Adult females and juveniles of both sexes want to handle and inspect the new infant. They pay particular attention to the infant's genitals and appear to be checking on its sex. Adult males are unlikely to handle new infants, but they frequently greet and grunt at new mothers, and may briefly touch the infant in passing.

Within a month or two, baboon infants become much more active and begin to explore their surroundings. They do not venture far from their mother, but if they do stray, their mother swiftly retrieves them so that they do not get themselves into trouble.

Once infants reach the age of three months, they have begun to lose their downy baby coat, and their fur becomes thicker and more like the adults' in color. This change occurs gradually. First, just their brows turn a yellow brown, followed by the fur around their wrists. Their face and ears gradually become much darker, and it is possible to tell the age of an infant baboon by the shade of its ears and its muzzle.

1

1. Very young infants spend up to 80 percent of their day suckling. They grow rapidly during the first few months of life.

2. At birth (a) baboons have pink faces and wrinkly noses. By 3 months (b) the face is grey with a pink tinge, and by 5-6 months (c) the pink and the wrinkles have gone.

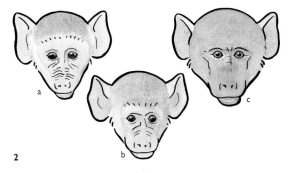

2

Weaning

By the age of five months, most infants have begun to feed themselves and have become less dependent on their mother's milk. They are more coordinated and physically stronger. As a result, they no longer spend so much time being carried around underneath their mother. Instead, they begin riding on their mother's back, jockey style, often using the base of the mother's tail as a support. They also spend more time away from their mother, playing with other infants and young juveniles, or feeding themselves. Once the infants have reached this more mobile stage, their mothers no longer pick them up when they want to move. Instead, a mother merely signals her intention to move by tapping the baby on the head, calling to it, or lowering her back. The infant then jumps into the normal travel position by itself.

By the age of six months or so, the infant is getting too large to be carried. Mothers tip their babies off when they jump on their backs, or grab and pull them off, often violently. This can produce loud squawks of protest from the infants at first, but they soon learn that they have to walk and they naturally start to follow their mother. Once the infants get to this stage, the mothers no longer signal to them when they are about to move. Instead, it is up to the infant to keep an eye on its mother and follow her.

By this point, infants are also spending less time suckling, and are making great strides in feeding themselves. Their mothers are less likely to let the infants suckle whenever they want to. Instead, the mother makes the infant wait until a convenient time when the infant will not be in the way, usually when she is resting or grooming. Some infants throw tantrums during their weaning period, objecting most strongly to being denied their

 CRYING FOR ATTENTION

Flowers are a good food for young baboons. They are soft and easy to pick and digest, but they are not always available. Among chacma baboons in the Western Cape of South Africa, the flowers fed on by young baboons die during the dry summer months. The adults rely on underground foods, but the infants have to return to suckling. When they are rejected by their mother, they throw tantrums until she lets them on the nipple. Crying for attention increases the amount of suckling they are allowed to do, and this enables them to survive through periods when they cannot fend for themselves.

1. (opposite) By the age of five months or so, an infant is well coordinated and is able to ride on its mother's back, instead of clinging to her chest.

1. A young infant clings to its mother's belly and suckles at the same time. Sometimes infants do not feed but merely hang onto the mother's nipple for extra support while they are carried.

2. Females with young infants frequently spend time together in a kind of "nursery club." The mothers often groom each other while their infants play.

mother's milk. The number of tantrums seems to depend on the quality of weaning foods, such as flowers or soft fruits, that are available. If these are plentiful, infants are less likely to make a fuss than when these foods are scarce. Infants are usually fully weaned by the age of 9 to 12 months, but this depends heavily on where in Africa they live.

The Drakensberg baboons

In the Drakensberg mountains of South Africa, chacma baboon infants continue to suckle well into their second year. Their mothers do not try to stop them from suckling and the infants have never been seen to throw tantrums. Drakensberg infants also learn to feed themselves more slowly. As a result of this slow development, females in the

Drakensberg have long intervals between successive births. They give birth once every three years. Most other baboons give birth every 18 to 24 months.

Conditions in the Drakensberg are harsh. Food is sparsely distributed and tends to be poor in quality. It is also a highly seasonal environment. All of this limits the ability of infant baboons to start feeding themselves. At the age when they would otherwise begin eating solid foods, around six months, Drakensberg infant baboons are faced with the winter months. During this time, foods suitable for young infants are unavailable. With nothing around to tempt them into independent feeding, the infants continue to suckle from their mothers. They can only begin to find their own food in the spring, six months later, when they are more than a year old. As a result, Drakensberg mothers invest far more care in their offspring than females in other baboon populations, and they produce fewer offspring. Despite the harsh conditions, this extra care actually increases their chance of survival relative to baboon infants in other populations. Drakensberg infants have a 95 percent chance of surviving to the age of two years, compared to 55 percent for some East African populations.

MOTHER-INFANT BEHAVIOR

Baboon mothers vary widely in the way they treat their offspring. Some females are casual, while others are rather over protective of their infants. First-time mothers, for example, are usually more protective of their infants than those who have had several offspring, probably because of their lack of experience. Differences between mothers can also be related to rank. High-ranking females are less

2

likely to be over protective than the low-ranking mothers. High-ranking females can afford to be more casual, since it is unlikely that their infants will suffer any harm at the hands of others. Other animals often show fear towards high-ranking infants and may try to avoid them when they approach, presumably because of the possible repercussions from the mother should any harm befall her offspring.

The same is not true for low-ranking females. Their offspring may be mistreated by higher-ranking females, and when this happens there is nothing the mother can do to protect them. A greater degree of protectiveness is understandable under these circumstances.

Infants can also be harmed even unintentionally. They may sometimes be kidnapped from their mothers by high-ranking juveniles or adults who carry them around with them, sometimes for hours. Even though they are well cared for during this time, they are unable to suckle and suffer severe dehydration. This can often be fatal. As a result, all baboon mothers, regardless of how casual or restrictive they are, usually show

1

2

great reluctance to let other baboons handle their infants or carry them away out of reach.

Mothering styles

While the more casual mothers seem to be happy for their infants to do their own thing, over-protective mothers are unwilling to let their infants stray at all, preferring to keep them in contact at all times. They are also reluctant to let other animals socialize with their infants. Infants of over-protective mothers are less likely to be groomed by other individuals during the first three months of life than infants whose mothers have a more relaxed attitude. Obviously, this has negative effects on the infant's development, since it has little opportunity to explore its environment, make friends, play, and

1. Infants attract a lot of attention from other animals in the group, especially juvenile and adult females.

2. A female inspects another's infant. Females often handle infants roughly, especially if the infant's mother is low-ranking.

Orphaned infant baboons are sometimes "adopted" by other troop members. They will usually survive, if they are capable of finding food for themselves.

generally begin to make sense of the social world that it has been born into. This can have a negative impact on the kind of personality the infant develops and its ability to interact with other animals once it is grown. On the other hand, infants of over-protective mothers are much less likely to come to any harm.

At Amboseli, in Kenya, yellow baboon infants of over-protective mothers are much less likely to die in the first few months after birth than the infants of casual mothers. However, because they reach independence much later than infants of casual mothers, over-protected infants are much less likely to survive if they are orphaned. Highly protective and less protective mothering styles seem to have complementary effects. While on the one hand encouraging infant independence ensures that infants will be able to take care of themselves if

disaster should strike, on the other hand it risks losing the infant completely because less care is being taken over its safety. Over-protective mothering makes it less likely that an infant will be able to face life on its own, but it increases the chance that the infant will actually make it through this critical period of infancy.

While maternal styles vary between individuals in the same group, there are also noticeable overall differences between populations. The olive baboon infants living in Gombe, in Tanzania, are more independent, more likely to be rejected or punished by their mothers, and receive less protection than the yellow baboon infants at Mikumi, another site in Tanzania. Gombe is a forested habitat, whereas Mikumi is savanna. It is possible that the greater availability of safe places to hide and the shorter distances moved each day in Gombe mean that

 FINDING FOOD

Acquiring feeding skills is a matter of trial and error. Unlike human parents, baboon mothers do not teach their youngsters how to find and process different foods. At first, young baboons are clumsy and slow at feeding. They do not realize that corms need to be dug out of the ground and often try to pull them out by force, usually with the result that the corm stays firmly underground and they are left clutching a useless stalk. As a result, young baboons usually feed on the scraps left behind by adults until they become more adept at digging for themselves.

1. (opposite) Infants start experimenting with solid food at around 2 to 3 months of age, although they do not start seriously feeding for themselves until around 6 to 7 months.

Previous page:
Infants often pick up feeding tips from adult baboons by feeding on the scraps the adults leave behind during foraging.

1

females can be more relaxed about what their infants are doing. Mikumi, by contrast, is open and the danger from predators is high, therefore mothers cannot allow infants the same freedom.

The same differences can be seen between different species of monkey, and between wild and captive populations. Mothers tend to be much more over-protective in the more-dangerous wild than they are in the safety of a captive environment. In the same way, baboons are less protective of their infants than monkeys who spend more of their time in the trees. Falling out of the tropical forest canopy obviously has dire consequences for an infant, and their mothers have to reduce the chance of this happening as best they can. Baboon infants spend most of their time on the ground, and are less likely to harm themselves if they fall off or

over things. Only at night, at sleeping trees or cliffs, is there any risk of an infant falling and injuring itself. As a result, mothers usually make sure that their offspring are snugly settled in their lap come nightfall.

Boys and girls

Male and female baboon infants show different patterns of development. This is partly due to differences in temperament. Female gelada infants, for example, seem to be much better than males at coordinating their behavior with that of their mother. They keep track of their mothers' movements more effectively and learn quickly that they should attempt to suckle only when their mothers are resting or grooming, rather than feeding. Female infants are generally more cautious than males and spend more time near their mother. This may allow them to learn their mothers' patterns of behavior more rapidly. Infant females are also more likely to be harassed by other adult females and this may encourage them to stay close to their mother.

Male infant baboons are much bolder. They stray farther from their mother at an earlier age and are more likely to play with infants and juveniles much older than themselves. It takes a male infant much longer to catch on to what its mother expects, so they can appear to be more demanding. In most cases, however, this is because they seek attention at an inappropriate time, not because they want more attention overall than female infants.

Both male and female infants of over-protective mothers take longer to mesh their behavior with their mothers' than the infants of casual mothers do. This might seem paradoxical, since over-protected infants spend more time with their mothers and should therefore learn more quickly. However, over protecting an infant inhibits its ability to learn. Rather than learning about their mothers' behavior, infants who are over protected learn instead that they have no control over what they want to do and they become frustrated. After a time, their response to over-protection is to stop trying to do things for themselves. As a result, the infants learn much more slowly, because they are no longer willing to investigate and explore new opportunities.

1. Among olive baboons, males often form strong attachments to particular infants. The infants usually belong to the male's group of "special friends."

2. A juvenile baboon "alarm calls" at a predator. As well as acquiring social skills, it is important for young baboons to learn survival skills.

2

Play behavior

Play is an important part of young baboons' development. It enables them to develop their strength and motor skills, and to learn the important social skills that they need later in life. Play is a useful way for young animals to learn about the world they live in, without coming to any harm. The amount of time they spend playing depends on the quality of the habitat. For example, young gelada baboons play much less and in a different way during the dry season than during the wet season. In the wet season, they are energetic, chasing and wrestling with each other. During the dry season, their play behavior tends to be much more low key, and they play more with objects, such as sticks, rather than with each other. This is because food is much scarcer during the dry season. At this time of year, gelada rely on corms

and rhizomes that grow underground, rather than the grass blades that form their wet season diet. Digging up corms is time consuming, and young baboons have to spend much more time feeding. As a result, they have little time left over for playing. More importantly perhaps, young baboons do not have enough energy to play. During the dry season they can only find enough food to keep them satisfied. As a result, energy-expending activities, such as play, have to be dropped.

While the ideal situation is for infants to have playmates of both sexes and all ages, in reality chance effects mean that this is unlikely. The number and sex of infants born into a baboon troop can fluctuate markedly from year to year. In extreme cases, only one infant may survive its first few months of life, or all the infants born will be of the same sex. Such imbalances have far-reaching consequences for the troop as a whole. During

 LIFE ON THE EDGE

Infancy is an uncertain period for baboons. In some populations, up to 50 percent of infants die in their first year of life. Often this is because of poor habitat conditions. Mothers cannot produce sufficient milk to feed their young and they die of malnourishment or disease. Predators kill infant baboons, and for gelada infants the weather can also have a big effect on survival. Like all baboons, gelada infants are born with a thin coat of soft, black hair. Infants born in the wet season are wet and cold almost all the time, and they die from chest infections and hypothermia.

1. (opposite) Play helps young animals to develop their muscles, build stamina, and increase their coordination.

1. Infant baboons are endlessly inquisitive. Even ordinary pebbles are a source of great interest, but this one's mother does not seem to agree.

2. Young infants show an interest in the outside world, although they may not be coordinated enough to take part in it.

years when only one or two infants are born, the infants do not have playmates of their own age and size. As a result, they end up playing with much larger juveniles. Being older and bigger, these animals tend to play much rougher games and treat younger infants as toys and playthings, rather than as playmates. As one might expect, this treatment can have consequences for the way these infants behave as adults. They are often more aggressive and less socially skilled than animals who grow up with play partners of the same age.

Similarly, if the sex ratio is unbalanced, a female infant may find herself with only male infants to play with, or vice versa. Males are generally bolder and rougher so that female infants tend to suffer at their hands. While a male who tries to play rough with a group of females is often rejected as a playmate and has to seek friends elsewhere. Again, these early experiences color the lives of such animals and effect the way they behave as adults.

Males who do not acquire the more subtle social skills that interacting with females bring, often find it hard to consort with females when they reach adolescence and adulthood. They tend to be too rough and aggressive, and this frightens the females off. The females are usually much better prepared for adulthood, even when they lack suitable playmates, because they have the example of their older female relatives to follow. Even so, they may still be clumsy socially if they have not had the intense training that playing with a larger group of boisterous infants and juveniles brings.

Among a group of yellow baboons in Amboseli, in Kenya, an imbalanced sex ratio resulted in a different kind of problem. Six out of the seven infants born in one year were female. While these baboons were young, this did not create a problem. However, when they reached three years old, all the females began to challenge the adults in rank-related contests, in order to establish themselves in the adult hierarchy. As a result, there was a period of chaos within the group. The rate of fighting increased dramatically and it became difficult for animals to keep track of just who was challenging, and who was supporting, whom. Thankfully, this period came to an end as soon as the females had established themselves in the adult hierarchy.

Young baboons and chimpanzees sometimes play together. However, this can be risky because chimpanzees hunt and eat baboons.

2

| 3 | **GROWING UP** |

COMING OF AGE

Female baboons reach maturity more rapidly than males. Females are classed as adult when they give birth to their first infant, at around seven years of age. Although they start menstruating at around 4 to 5 years of age, young females do not actually release eggs from their ovaries and are incapable of becoming pregnant. This period between starting menstruation and getting pregnant is referred to as "adolescent sterility."

Males, by contrast, reach puberty much later than females and only become fully adult at around 8 to 9 years of age. This is due to the large difference in size between males and females. Although males are capable of fertilizing females by about 5 to 6 years of age, it takes them another two years or so to reach their full adult body size. As they cannot compete effectively against other males until they are full size adults, it takes male baboons much longer than female baboons to start their reproductive careers.

Male baboons undergo an adolescent growth spurt when they hit puberty. They suddenly shoot up, growing rapidly and soon outstripping adult females in body size. Their large canine teeth begin growing at this time as well, and they start to acquire the capes and manes that characterize adult male baboons. During this period, with their hormones in turmoil, males begin to assert their dominance over each other and over adult females. Adolescent males can be unpredictable, and if there are several males reaching puberty at the same time, life can become rather fraught as they learn to

1

1. Juvenile female baboons groom adult females as a way of breaking into the social network of the adults.

2. A baboon confronts a jackal. Young male baboons are more vulnerable to attacks by predators as they emigrate and wander around alone looking for a new group to join.

⭐ A single male baboon is capable of driving off an adult leopard.

assert themselves. Adult females seem to have the hardest time of it. While the males are juveniles, females are able to dominate them if they outrank the male's mother. However, once the males reach adolescence and are both larger and physically stronger than females, they begin to challenge the status quo. Whenever females try to displace them at a feeding site, they refuse to budge and may even aggressively attack a female if she persists. Gradually, with more than a few protests from the females, the adolescent males come to dominate all the females, and acquire a rank just below the adult males in the troop.

Seeking pastures new

It is usually around the time of adolescence that males leave their home troops to look for pastures new. They may come into conflict with the adult males in their troop, but this is relatively rare. Male baboons leave of their own accord and are not forced out of the group by the resident adult males. By adolescence, males have become increasingly isolated from their mothers and other female relatives. As youngsters, males spend a lot of time grooming their mothers, but this gradually declines as they become older, although their mothers will still spend just as much time grooming them.

When males leave their home troops, they often take some time to make the break. They may wander off for a few days, but they are likely to return to the home troop and stay there for a while. The periods away from home get longer and longer, until one day the male just does not come back. For the lucky majority, this means that they have started a new life in a troop elsewhere, but for the not-so-lucky, their absence may be due to attack by a predator while they are alone and vulnerable.

2

Networking

Adolescence is the time when young females start integrating themselves into the adult network and finding their place in the hierarchy of the group. Young female chacma baboons begin to form coalitions with each other around this time, and help to defend each other against attack by their peers. They also start directing their grooming towards high-ranking adults, possibly to secure their support as they attempt to achieve a high rank. Adolescents are much more likely than adults to initiate grooming with unrelated females. They are also more willing to groom, even when they get nothing in return. Most grooming encounters between adolescents and adults are one-sided, with the younger female doing all the grooming.

Once they begin menstruating, young females are usually established in the dominance hierarchy, but are not necessarily popular. This changes with the birth of their first infant. Young mothers seem to take advantage of the grooming opportunities that motherhood provides to bring themselves more fully into the troop. Among one population of chacma baboons in the Western Cape, a young female migrated into a troop after most of her own troop died in an epidemic. For a long time, only juveniles and adolescent males would groom her. But once she gave birth, things changed almost overnight. She was groomed by most of the adult females, and groomed them in return. Some of these grooming bonds persisted after her son grew past the attractive stage, and today no one would know she had not been born and bred in this troop.

1. Mothers are often protective of their infants, but will sometimes allow other individuals to groom their babies.

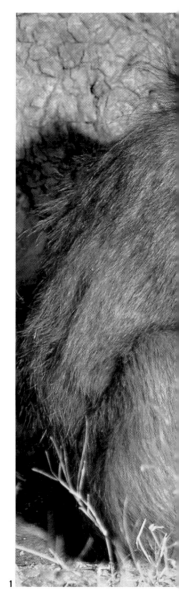

AGGRESSION AND CONFLICT

AGGRESSION AND CONFLICT

Living in a group inevitably leads to aggression and conflict at times. After all, different individuals have different goals and interests. Baboons have a reputation for being particularly aggressive animals, but this assumption does them an injustice. Males are competitive and aggressive with each other, but this is because the stakes are high in the mating game. However, their relationships with females and infants testify to a softer side.

Female baboons tend to be more relaxed than males, although they are not afraid to fight. Group life is a balance between hostility and peace. Baboons must not only make sure they are not exploited or outcompeted by their group mates, but they also have to maintain group harmony. Balancing the costs and benefits of group life requires a variety of social skills and tactics, all of which help to make baboon life complex and endlessly fascinating.

Previous page: An adult male baboon yawns as part of a threat display and shows off his impressive canine teeth.

MATE COMPETITION

In baboon groups, adult females always outnumber males by at least two to one. In both gelada and hamadryas baboons, the ratio may be much higher, and a single male will have exclusive mating rights with up to 10 females. In other savanna baboons, the number of males in a group depends on the number of females. Males tend to be distributed across the groups in a population in a way that equalizes their mating opportunities. When males emigrate to new groups, they tend to move from groups with a high ratio of males to female to those with a higher number of females. As a result, the males end up with more or less the same potential for mating. Males in big groups have more mating opportunities available to them, but face more competition from other males. Males in small groups have fewer mating opportunities since there are fewer females available, but they face less competition to get those matings.

If groups are small, there will be only a single male. Small groups of females are easy for a single male to control because the chance that more than one female will be fertile at any one time is low. Other males will not attempt to join a small group if their chance of mating is unlikely, and, therefore, they go elsewhere. As groups grow larger, however, the chance that more than one female will be ready to mate increases substantially. When this happens, a male finds himself in a difficult situation because he cannot be in two places at

1. A male baboon is barking as he chases off a rival. Aggression between males is common in baboon groups.

once. While he is busy defending and mating with one female, the attentions of the other female can be monopolized by another male. As a result of these increased mating opportunities, other males join the troop. Once this happens, the males have to fight to decide who gets to mate with the females as they become fertile.

Signals and threats

Competition over mates is a major issue for baboon males. Battles over females can be intense, violent, and prolonged. Male baboons signal aggression with a number of facial expressions. A raising of the eyebrows while staring straight at an opponent is considered a threat, as is exaggerated yawning. This shows off the male's canines to his opponents and lets them know he means business. A variant on this theme is the "lip flipping" of male gelada. Their upper lips are mobile and can be flipped back up over their noses to reveal an intimidating set of teeth. Subordinate males in receipt of such threats may "fear grimace" and present their rear to the aggressive male. They will also lean aside whenever a dominant male passes, or even jump out of the way. If actual fighting breaks out, males slash at each other with their large canine teeth. They usually go for the heads of their opponents, and most wounds are found on the muzzle and neck. These can range from superficial flesh wounds and

★ Hamadryas males respect the relationships that other males have with females. If a male spots a male-female pair grooming together, he will not attempt to interact with the female himself.

1

1. Males' canine teeth are razor sharp. They keep them that way by grinding them against a specially adapted tooth in the lower jaw.

2. A baboon that has been threatened by another makes a "fear grimace" and seeks comfort from a more friendly baboon.

2

tears to deep puncture wounds. Wounds to the arms and shoulders are also common. One old chacma baboon in the Western Cape, South Africa, had half his tail bitten off during a prolonged fight with a much younger male. The recovery powers of baboons are astounding, however. Within 24 hours of a fight, a male's wounds will have dried up considerably and already begun to heal.

The scars that many males bear on their muzzles, broken fingers, and missing teeth, all indicate just how seriously males take their mating prospects. In gelada and hamadryas baboons, males fight over entire units of females. In gelada, young males without harems live together in all-male bands.

They are constantly on the lookout for harems that they can take over from the resident male. Often the young males attack a resident male in a kind of relay race. In turn they chase, fight, and harass the resident male until he is exhausted. Each of the young males remains relatively fresh because they can get some rest in between bouts of aggression. Once the resident male's defenses are down, one of the younger males will challenge him to a decisive takeover fight for possession of the harem. However, the success of the takeover ultimately lies with the females. If they do not like the look of the new male, no matter how strong and virile he appears, they refuse to accept him as their new

1

1. Two baboon males fighting. These fights can often result in serious injuries with males scarred for life.

leader and stick with the original male. Larger harems tend to be easier to take over than small ones because the resident male is unable to pay enough attention to all his females. As a result, they have less loyalty toward the resident male and are more likely to favor a newcomer.

Consortships

Unlike gelada, savanna baboons have to fight over females on a day-to-day basis. When females are fertile the males form consort relations with them, staying close by and stopping other males from getting too close. Again, it is the females who have the final decision. If a female does not want to be consorted by a particular male, she will scream whenever he approaches, and may often run away and hide. It is the females who have the final say about a male's mating success.

Among savanna baboons, dominant males are usually the most successful at mating. They are able to beat off other males more effectively, and females often prefer them to other males. Lower-ranking males do not simply accept this, however. Among the East African yellow and olive baboons, males team up with each other to form "coalitions" and use their combined force to break up consortships.

Coalition formation means that male consortships are short in olive and yellow baboons, lasting only a few hours. In contrast, South African chacma baboon males can maintain consortships for up to a week at a time. This is because chacma males do not form coalitions. In chacma baboons,

1. A female olive baboon presents to an approaching male. Males are always dominant to females in baboon society.

2. A male hamadryas with his group of females. Males often have to protect their females from harassment from other animals, both male and female.

consort takeovers happen peacefully at sleeping sites. A female arrives with one male in the evening and leaves with another in the morning. Other males seem to respect consortships and do not try to harass the male or interact with the female. One suggestion is that chacma males live in tougher habitats than their East African counterparts and do not have spare energy to engage in costly and possibly unsuccessful fighting over females.

Hamadryas males also form consortships with the females in their units. When a male is consorting, he engages in a highly ritualized form of greeting behavior with potential rival males. This behavior is the same as the notifying behavior that males use when they are trying to decide on the direction of departure from sleeping cliffs. Consorting males approach rivals, moving with a distinctive swinging gait, and the two males engage in various greeting behaviors such as lip smacking and presenting their rear.

It has been suggested that the consorting male engages in this behavior in order to stop tensions developing between him and other males. They direct friendly behavior toward other males in order to reestablish relations that might be heading toward a fight over the female. Greeting also allows males to assess each other's strength and to make a more informed decision about whether they should fight or not. A rival male who refuses to present his rear to a consorting male is indicating that he may prove to be trouble in the near future, while a consorting male who frequently uses greeting behavior to all his rivals shows that he is feeling vulnerable and threatened by other males. Males can then use these clues to decide whether they are likely to be successful if they fight for a consortship.

MALES AND INFANTS

One extreme form of male competition over mates is infanticide, or the killing of infants. In some savanna baboon populations, new males entering a group for the first time will occasionally kill young infants because it brings the dead infant's mother back into a state where she is ready to mate. While she is suckling her infant, the mother will not be able to become pregnant again because the

2

production of hormones needed for the growth and release of eggs from the ovaries ceases. In the normal course of events, a mother returns to reproductive condition 9 to 12 months after birth, once the infant is weaned and eating solid foods. The death of an infant puts an end to suckling and allows the mother's reproductive hormones to begin in again much earlier. Males are able to compete effectively for mates only during the few years that they are in their prime, and by killing an infant, a male can mate with its mother much more quickly than if he waited for the infant to be weaned. With the death of her infant, the only way for the female to recoup her loss is to mate with the male and have another infant as quickly as possible.

Deflecting aggression

The tendency toward infanticide among some male baboons could explain another unusual aspect of male behavior. When a male baboon gets into an aggressive situation with another male, he will sometimes pick up and carry a small infant, often presenting it to his opponent. It is thought that the presence of the infant somehow protects the male against any further aggression.

More surprisingly, in one population of chacma baboons in Botswana, males were found to carry infants that they were likely to have fathered, especially when their opponent was a newcomer to the group. As a result, it was suggested that males

1. An olive baboon male yawns in a threatening manner. When consorting with fertile females, males often face aggression from rival males.

2. An adult male gelada stands on his hind legs to scan for danger. Males have to be alert for attacks by other males, as well as by predators.

were trying to protect their infants from infanticide by the new male. This is possible, although such behavior does seem risky. After all, the male is directly putting the infant in danger. Another suggestion is that placing the infant in danger is, in fact, the male's intention. By bringing his own infant into the fray, the male is giving a signal that he will be prepared to fight to prevent the infant from getting injured. In effect, the male is trying to call the other male's bluff and stop a real fight from developing. The presence of the infant may also act in a more immediate sense. Young infants, with their black coats and pink faces, bring out a nurturing response in adult animals. The sudden arrival of an infant may help defuse an aggressive situation by producing this response in the male's opponent, so that his aggression toward the male is diluted and he is less likely to want to fight. Whatever the reason, the strategy is effective. In most cases, the opponent backs down.

2

A living shield

Males may also use infants to secure the support of females. If an infant is threatened, it is common for the infant's mother and her relatives to chase and attack the threatening individual. Gelada baboon males use infants to signal to their rivals that, if they continue to pick a fight, they are likely to face the wrath of the infant's mother and all her kin. Young "follower" males are most likely to behave this way. These are males that attach themselves to another male's harem, without attempting to take over by aggressive means. Generally the two males get along in a peaceful manner. However, if aggression does break out, and the harem holder threatens the follower male, then the follower will quickly grab an infant in order to force the harem holder to back down. Although the harem holder is usually more powerful, even he cannot withstand a concerted attack by all the females in his harem. The success of this strategy means that one of the first things young follower males do when entering a harem is to form a relationship with a female who has an infant. The infant wants to be around the male, and the male himself encourages it, so that his small living shield is always at hand when needed.

BATTLES BETWEEN GROUPS

Baboons are not territorial in the way that most forest-living monkeys are. They do not attempt to defend an area against other baboon groups. In fact, baboon home ranges tend to overlap each other extensively. However, it is unusual for more than one baboon group to be in the same area at exactly the same time. Groups seem to try to avoid each other as much as possible. This may help to reduce competition for food, which is important from the females' point of view, however, it is males who show the strongest response to strange groups, and this seems to be linked to protecting their mating rights. Males are known to attempt to mate with fertile females from another troop, while young females will also seek out matings with strange males if they are given the opportunity. As a result,

males are sensitive to the risk posed by males from other troops, and so they take action to avoid other troops where possible.

In the Drakensberg mountains of South Africa, chacma males in groups with more females than average sometimes respond to the presence of another group by rounding up and herding away their own females. An extra male joining the group would increase the level of competition for them, so they try to keep their troop at a distance. When they discover that they are heading straight for another group, they change direction so that the groups do not come into contact at close quarters. These decisions are often made when they are up to 4.5 miles away, something which the high visibility of the mountain habitat makes possible. This confirms that males anticipate future risk since groups at that distance do not present an immediate threat.

 COPULATION CALLS

When female baboons mate, they produce a series of loud grunts known as a copulation call. When other males hear the call, they are alerted to the fact that the female is fertile, and may attempt to mate with her as well. It has been suggested that females do this to ensure that they get a good-quality father for their offspring. Only the males best at fighting off the opposition will get the chance to mate. Alternatively, females may be trying to reduce the risk of infanticide. Mating with many males one after the other means that they all have a chance of being the offspring's father and therefore later they cannot risk killing an infant that might be theirs. Neither of these arguments seems to apply to chacma baboons, however. Females tend to have long-lasting consortships with single males, and other males do not get the chance to mate.

Conflicts between females

Females seem much less concerned about other troops than males. Most of their tensions and conflicts arise within their own groups, and their level of aggression also depends on where in Africa they live. Mountain chacma baboons and gelada baboon females are low-key when it comes to aggression. Because they eat grass, which is plentiful and widespread, disputes over food are rare. Baboon females in other habitats show much higher rates of aggression. Females in the Mkuzi game reserve, in South Africa, for example, have at least one aggressive interaction with another female every hour. At Mkuzi, a lot of the food that the baboons feed on grow on trees and bushes.

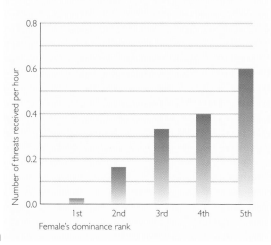

FEMALE AGGRESSION

1

1. Low-ranking female baboons receive far more threats from other females than do high-ranking females.

2. In this baboon fight the animal on the left adopts a submissive posture toward the more dominant animal on the right.

2

These are patchily distributed in the environment and found only in certain areas. Because all the food is clumped into a single tree or bush, it is easy for one or two dominant animals to monopolize the entire food supply for themselves and keep other baboons out. As a result, females need to fight for their right to gain access to these high-quality foods.

Most conflicts between females tend to be short lived and are dominance related. High-ranking females will often attack subordinates who refuse to relinquish their feeding sites, for example. In some cases, males will intervene in females' fights and put a stop to them, usually by chasing one or both of the females away. Sometimes this male is the "special friend" of one of the females, but in some cases the dominant male will intervene without having a particularly strong relationship with either of the females. In most cases, male intervention prevents any further aggression between the two females.

Peace-making

Given all the aggression that can exist within baboon groups, they would soon descend into chaos without some way of keeping the peace. Females, in particular, are good at making up again after fights. These acts of reconciliation are important for the individuals concerned; they allow animals to call a truce and signal that they will not attack each other again (for the time being, anyway). This is crucial because aggression increases stress levels and can have far-reaching consequences for the animal concerned. Baboons with high levels of stress hormones are less likely to conceive and more likely to suffer infection and disease. In the short term, they are likely to be more tense and twitchy because they are uncertain whether they are about to be attacked again, and this can reduce their efficiency at their daily tasks, such as feeding.

Scientists can gauge the level of stress animals experience by measuring the amount of "self-directed behavior" that they show. Self-directed behavior refers to things such as scratching and self-grooming. Humans show similar kinds of behavior when faced with an uncomfortable situation: biting one's nails is the classic example. Baboons react similarly, and researchers have found that the amount of such behavior that baboons show is a reliable index of how stressed they are. For example, after two baboons have had a fight, their rate of

scratching increases until they have made up with their former opponent. Measuring the amount of scratching thus gives scientists some insight into how baboons feel about certain situations.

When dominant and subordinate animals groom, for example, the lower-ranking partner will often display evidence that it feels stressed, despite the friendly nature of the grooming behavior. This is not the case for two closely ranked individuals, however, suggesting that there is something different about the nature of grooming between equals, compared to grooming between dominants and subordinates.

To defuse a stressful situation, female savanna baboons signal reconciliation by grunting at each other. This is unusual, as most other monkeys use grooming or some other form of physical contact to achieve reconciliation. Following an aggressive

1. Many threat displays are bluffs. Males use them in an attempt to avoid real aggression.

2. Sometimes bluffing does not work and a real fight breaks out. Females as well as males can get involved in prolonged battles, although females tend to do less damage to each other than males.

2

1

interaction, one of the two females involved will approach the other and softly grunt at her. This tends to occur soon after the original attack, sometimes only a minute or two after the fight has ended. Once this peaceful contact has been established, the likelihood that the females will attack each other again in the short term is greatly reduced. The females also become much more relaxed and the amount of self directed behavior that they show drops.

The value of reconciliation depends on the relationship between the females. Baboon females are particularly likely to achieve reconciliation with high-ranking opponents and mothers with young infants. This may be because these individuals can offer certain benefits: high-ranking females may allow them access to feeding sites, while mothers may exchange grooming for infant handling.

1. Grooming can be used to calm down animals after aggressive incidents and restore peace between two individuals.

2. Living in close proximity with other animals can often be stressful. Baboons have special behavioral mechanisms to keep stress levels low.

 BODY LANGUAGE

Baboons use a variety of postures and facial expressions to communicate with each other. When a baboon sees another animal that it wants to interact with, it often makes what is known as the "come-hither" face. The baboon will pull its ears back against its head while raising its eyebrows and smacking its lips together. Lip smacking is common in all sorts of friendly interactions, such as between young infants and their mothers, or while grooming. Males may also lip smack when attempting to attract fertile females. Female baboons will also touch each other on the side, or even embrace to signal friendliness. Males do not go this far, but olive baboon males demonstrate their trust of each other by briefly handling or "diddling" each other's testicles.

Family values

Within baboon society, making-up after aggression is essential, so that animals can continue to live together in peace and reap the benefits of group life. While it is true that baboons can be noisy and intimidating, most aggressive behavior is bluff. In particular, baboons will only threaten or attack humans if they are cornered and can see no other escape. Aggression and dominance play a key role in structuring baboon society, and are the behaviors that catch an observer's eye, but social skills are always more effective than brute force. It is ironic that baboons are often considered to be aggressive and dangerous animals when their lives are characterized by close family relationships, care of the young and intense socializing. Understanding baboons, then, means understanding many of the features of our own social lives. Family values have been important for much longer than we realize.

2

FURTHER INFORMATION

BOOKS

Jeanne Altmann, *Baboon Mothers and Infants* (Harvard University Press, 1980)
A detailed account of a study of mother-infant behavior among the baboons of Amboseli, Kenya.

John Fleagle, *Primate Adaptation and Evolution* (Academic Press, New York, 1988)
Covers all aspects of anatomy, behavior and evolution.

Hans Kummer, *In Quest of the Sacred Baboon* (Princeton University Press, 1995)
An autobiographical account of Hans Kummer's field-based studies of the hamadryas baboon.

Eugene Marais, *The Soul of the Ape* (Penguin Books, 1979)
Eugene Marais was probably the first person to study baboons in their natural habitat. Although a number of his theories have not stood the test of time, this book remains an engaging read.

Alison Richard, *Primates in Nature* (W. H. Freeman and Company, New York, 1985)
A textbook account of primate ecology and lifestyles.

Barbara Smuts, *Sex and Friendship in Baboons* (Aldine, New York, 1985)
A detailed description and explanation of "special friendships" in olive baboons in Kenya.

Karen Strier, *Primate Behavioral*

Ecology (Allyn and Bacon, 2000)
Applies the most up-to-date theories to explain behavior across the primate order.

Shirley Strum, *Almost Human* (Elm Tree Books 1987)
An autobiographical account of a pioneering long-term baboon study in Kenya.

MAGAZINE

BBC Wildlife Magazine
A monthly look at wildlife and conservation world wide.

WEBSITES

America Society of Primatologists
http://www.asp.org

Fauna and Flora International
http://www.ffi.org.uk

International Primate Protection League
http://www.ippl.org/index.html

International Primatological Society
http://indri.primate.wisc.edu/pin/ips.html

Jane Goodall Institute
http://www.janegoodall.org/index.html

Primate Conservation
http://www.primate.org

Primate Society of Great Britain
http://www.ana.ed.ac.uk/PSGB/home.html

INDEX

Italic type denotes illustrations